To my beautiful, own,
Maene-annie.

I love you with all my heart.

I feel pretty broken when
we're apart.

This book sparks my imagination.

♡ Joey

Christmas 2012

P.S.
I think you might be Ramona
(what a fabulous name)

no planets strike josh bell

University of Nebraska Press
Lincoln and London

© 2004 by Josh Bell
Manufactured in the United States of America
⊗
First Nebraska paperback printing: 2008

Library of Congress Cataloging-in-Publication Data
Bell, Josh, 1971–
No planets strike / Josh Bell.
p. cm.
ISBN 978-0-8032-2040-9 (pbk.: alk. paper)
I. Title.
PS3602.E64546N6 2008
811'.6—dc22 2008014708

Acknowledgments

Many thanks to the editors of the publications in which these poems appeared, sometimes in slightly different form:

Boston Review, Canary, Can We Have Our Ball Back?, Chiron, Colorado Review, Exquisite Corpse, Fence, Gulf Coast, Hotel Amerika, Iowa Review, Jubilat, Madison Review, Mudfish, Nerve, Painted Bride Quarterly, Perihelion, Prairie Schooner, Slope, Sycamore Review, Verse, Volt, and *Words on Walls.*

"Zombie Sunday (the stars swing in like buccaneers)" is for Matt Guenette.
"A Note on the Type" is for Andy Smith.

All the rest are for my wonderful parents, without whose love and support none of this was possible, and for my grandmother, who always told me so.

Two fellowships facilitated the writing of these poems: the Paul Engle Postgraduate Fellowship from the University of Iowa, and the Diane Middlebrook Fellowship from the University of Wisconsin's Creative Writing Institute. My gratitude to those donors and decision makers.

Gracious thanks to Indiana State University (Pete Carino, Matt Brennan). Thanks to the lovely and inimitable Rodney Jones. Thanks to Southern Illinois University at Carbondale (Beth Lordan and Andy Curtis, Gloria Jones, Sean Chapman, Jon Ritz). Thanks to Mark Beagle, Susan Sharp, and Bob Myers. Thanks to the University of Iowa Writers' Workshop (Jim, Jorie, and Marvin) for their time and wisdom. Thanks to the University of Wisconsin's Creative Writing Institute (Barry, Kercheval, Wallace) for the same. Thanks to Tim Donnelly, for the kind assist. Thanks to Aliki Barnstone, Joel Brouwer, Ashley Capps, Jim Cummins, Tim Earley, Matt Guenette, Sophia Kartsonis, Cate Marvin, Donald Revell, and Bruce Smith for their help and suggestions. Thanks to Erin Belieu for pulling this book from the general hedgerow, and thanks to all the writers whose lines I have misquoted or stolen.

Table of Contents

Coming Attractions

First the poem wherein the poem speaks to other poems.
Then the poem wherein the poem speaks to the reader, and is waylaid.

Then the poem which begins: "9 out of 10 women/who have saved my life
    agree/that I start breathing/like a champion."
Then with some whimsical poems of regret. Then certain "Songs of Abstinence"

followed closely by the poem mourning the fellatio embargo of 1993.
Next the poem about love indivisible. Now a certain number of untitled poems.

Then a rondel entitled "A Rondel." A sonnet entitled "A Sonnet."
A sestina entitled "A Ghazal for Uncle Mike." Then 34 poems beginning with
    the word "I."

Then the poem endlessly rejected, followed by "The Little Poem Who Tastes
    Like a Hospital."
Now another poem about love. A poem implanted. The poem of scorched
    milk and bees.

The poem recumbent. The poem retarded. The poem rhadamantine. The dictionary
    poem.
The poem of daily manifestos. The poem who stutters, who finds not love.

Then with the "Poem Coming Out of My Ears." Then the untouchable poem
and the furbearing poem. The barnstorming poem and the poem your mother
    warned you about,

the poem which ends with the line "and that's the thing/that really cracks
    me up/about chaos theory."
Next a poem ruthlessly co-opted by the insidious concerns of The State.

Subsequently a poem entitled "Get Your Greasy Hands Off My Porsche, Walt
    Whitman."
Now the darkling poem. The Aperture. The Dragon's Stepchild. The Kundalini
    Oblongatta.

The Clinch. Now the poem in which my fly has been down for over 2000 years.
The poem unmanned. The never ending poem and the poem that never began.

A dolphin safe poem. The poem without conscience or comma.
The poem which explains everything while you're sleeping.

The poem you lived with once. The poem that dropped from the sky and is known
as "The Last Poem" or the "There is No Such Poem as *This* Poem" poem.

The Beautiful American Poem

Some slob tracked burning styrofoam across the dear sky's parlor
and Airstream trailers run silver and mindless across 80
toward Nebraska like minnows down a drainpipe.
If all this, our stalled-on-the-shoulder, floorboard love,
amounts to more than heat-waves or jerky strips,
I'll quit talking about the architecture of Quik Trips
and I'll plant a moon pie in the median and when we return
next May to see its wet, alien stalks,
I'll wonder at the days we've seen. Jesus, baby, the days that we have seen.
I know a woman who in one weekend
slept with *Jane's Addiction* and a trucker from Moline.
There have been times I needed a ride more than anything.
America is the brave way to take a beating.
A beating is the shy way to say "I love you."
An exit ramp reaches easily into the Methodist fields.
Two gentlemen wrestle a weed-whacker out of Turnbull's Tavern
at 1pm, and an old lady mows her lawn on a John Deere.
That thing on her head is a bonnet, for the sun, and this is Oxford, Iowa.
Shoot me with a gun, please. I have finally decided to show my face here
and I want you to shoot me in it, with a gun, please.
They say that sometimes up on the silos
your eyes take on the wind's perspective,
and you come floating down out of the clouds
like something thought-out and beautiful,
and the way you see the fields is truly something else,
and the way you move the trees,
and the people are flannel tongues, inching, mouthless,
of their own, on patches of field, and here. Rivers.
I'll quit talking of people as tongues and rivers as brown,
flashing legs, and I'll quit talking if you put your fingers to my lips.
The wind is up there, and looking down hard, you can bet.
Whatever's better than love gets you drunk and wrestling weed-whackers.
Whatever's better than that, you spit down your chin for.

Sleeping with Artemis

I hadn't been that ashamed since
the Spartiate festival of the Hyacinthids,
and it was harder than we thought, sleeping
with Artemis. We brought sandwiches;
she brought arrows and stuck them
fletching up in the sand. We were vastly
unequipped. I looked to the heavens,
like you will, and asked for guidance
and a shield. To no avail. Furthermore,

the wine didn't help like we thought.
She drank it down, cursed our mothers,
and only got reckless, really, popped
the blister on her heel, drew the bow,
and, with both eyes shut, skewered
Crissippus. We scattered like snacks.
I believe it happened in that clearing
by the stream, where much transpired
as of late: two dead last April—the girl

who smoked flowers—that quiet kid who
turned into bark. We should have known
better, with the storied plants along the bank
and the instructive constellations in the sky.
Then she swept up out of the hedge like
a jack-knifed lion, a moon on each shoulder,
but you read the report. Indeed, sir,
we felt hairless, the offspring of mice,
when she quoted Hemingway, then turned
the forest to her wishes: leaves dropped

like bombs: branches shook: and where
the hounds came from, no one can tell.
From time to time, picking us apart now
from the stream, knee-deep and eyeing
the rushes for movement, she'd glance down
to her shirt, but it was always someone
else's blood. I remember her teeth
weren't as straight as you'd think.
But something about her was perfect.

Zombie Sunday

Gentle handed holy father, or whomever,
we have ways of making you talk,
and I am tired of your illustrious distractions,
the sunlight, the hortatory sex, the Marcel Proust
and all those pulsing vegetables
you've hidden in the garden, and when I hear a certain piece of music,
the kind invented by your better children
to replace the load-bearing voices
we misplaced so long ago—that professional and wingéd chorus
once strong, now trembling and withdrawn
to a drizzling echo in barrels of sludge
buried behind the supermarket,
the angelic orders individually wrapped
in garbage bags and vibrating out of whack
in watery ditches on the sides of highways—
your sad and higher class of road-kill—
and when I hear that certain piece of music
built to replace them, and, for an instant,
can hear fingers brushing across strings,
slender fingers, or hear that sharp,
vulnerable intake of breath before singing,
the breath which gathers up the shapeless air
and drags it down the throat and back,
different now, beautiful, a clean sound
like a clear piece of tile which perfectly fits
the space the lungs pulled it from,
then fades back into nothing, and the same air
can be breathed over and over
and sung again, different voices or the same,
your dirty wedding song or hateful lullaby,
and when I hear this certain piece of music,
what is the stroke of faltering light
that flashes across the hearer's closing eye?
There's a word for it, just as there's a word
for this tree I crouch behind, waiting
for someone to pass, the white bark like cigarette-paper
and these pallid roots, whose each subtle declension I am studying.
I'm afraid it is you, hiding or seeking,
pulsing in the down-beats, riding with us
through the rests, glowing white

like phosphorescent algae on the singer's tongue,
you gathering up a responsible speed in the human lung
and coming out a scream which combs the moon,
like a knot of hair, bleeding from the trees.
Lastly, I thank you for this morning's latest headache,
which is a good one, as you know,
a piece of work you must be proud of,
this ugly siren toward which all cares
are drawn and annihilated, as once a sudden violin
I heard coming from a basement radio
a million years ago, stood up through the coda
then engulfed it, like a golem waking in a forest
to breakfast on the throbbing trees.
Send me more cudgelings, more suppurations,
the very awful kind that tamed your seething martyrs
into glory, the masterful flourishes
and gristled fret-works which caused the chosen few
to take it, and when they took it, like it.
But this is your kind of speech, now, isn't it,
you with the spirits in moraine about your boat-like feet?
I'm tired of the several wonders, the bland musics,
the universal weeping, the human songs
made of lost words that twitch and ache like phantom limbs.
You should have left me to my own devices,
which are legendary, spider-like, and fashioned
from rusted fence-wire, then thrown mine body unto kites.
How do you do it? How should we resist?
Let me never plead to imp my tongue
to the likes of yours, which speaks planets into orbit,
for have I not been afflicted with the Earth, barely spinning as it is?
And won't your words come limping back
from the former void to help us fall apart
in the arranged directions, piece by piece,
like any good orchestra, some words now,
please, even with their several meanings spattered
by the gone machinery of others I have lost?

A Meditation Concerned with What You Might Be Meditating About, Ramona

A picture's worth a thousand worms, Ramona.
The stars are the vestigial nipples of our Lord.
Darling, you have clipped the hedges even thrice
since I parked my shaving kit in your medicine cabinet,
and it's time for us to speak, yet gently, again, about
how very much I mean to you. Mumbledy-peg,
Ramona. Ramona, Ramona, and the sky flung out
above your pointed shoulders like a knapsack
unfastened or a river with the hiccups. Excuse me.
You move through hallways like a water-bug on fire.
You slide down the conversation like guts down
a rooftop. Move the river to fit you. Suck all
nipples on the underbelly closest to your heart.
Fluff the pillows for the skip-tracers of your love
so they'll be comfy while they wait for you
to make good on the bonds you have signed for.
You will find most of this information in books.
You think too much about Roman emperors.
Roman emperors, and their sly corrupted bellies.
I renewed my subscription to *American Hand-gunner*.
At least I heard your bluebird sing, is a song lyric.
Sometimes I wish I was Catholic, is another.
You're thinking, I left a note inside a ship inside a bottle
for his mother, for when I kill him during
reindeer games and have to flee the country.
You think that's how she'll know to bury me
standing up. I say, *I* say, height lasts longer than
ambition. Much of what you think doesn't
move me. Much of what you think, you don't
tell me, Ramona, Ramona, you hardly live
in the suburbs in a white house. I have hunted
in the hedgerows for clues to your inner life
and I have hunted big game in your kitchen.
I fucked around and shot the pork roast.
The juvenile pork roast is considered a delicacy
in some regions, was my totally brilliant excuse.
I hate you. You love a spoon and someone else.
The sky's so gorgeous and tubby tonight even
an earthworm could put you on its back, and fly.

My Week as a Pornographic Film Queen

I am aware of the time
and what passes through me,

which are fevers and wings.
I am smarter than the newspaper,

Tony, and I am that lovely girl
who should be going down, February

blond, a phone number pressed
between the pages of a book,

feet like tropical fish, and I am a magnet,
a way South, the heat that starts

out from your shoulder-blades
and settles in your spine, a chill.

Today, the legacy of meat
is a bride. I am a bride, how

do I look? It doesn't mean
anything. You were gone, I was

waiting in the K mart parking lot.
Like a couple of trees, we weren't

there for each other. I come
with chemicals and a net,

and like a grubby girl-child
with a hanger twisted

around her neck, I'll make it count.
Like a young man in a dark

cubicle, I'll moan like the batteries
were included. Buy me

a pretty white hat and buy me
another pretty white hat.

One to scrape my eyes into
and one to cover them up with.

Dear Song

A girl like you once showed me how
the moon committed suicide.
She put on her make-up, stepped from her shoes, laid down in bed, and lived.
Why should I be the moon, she said, and she cried.
We looked up at the stars. Then we looked up at the stars.
White, tiny, smart, vicious, the stars, the stars, the stars.
I started this letter fifteen times, but I could only end it once;
I was up all last night, sleeping.
A woman like you once showed me how
to euthanize the stars,
but there is no one like you
to teach me how to wake, yet I'm sure I heard
the waves, the telepathic sea-gulls,
and whatever creature of guilt the voice of semi trucks belongs to, there,
screaming over the bridge next door,
the bridge beneath the stars.
But outside, it does what it does,
Virginia Beach, Thanksgiving week,
and there are no new bridges to jump from.
It's all been done. Every night new stars arrive to watch the old bridge
next door, where the same people gather on ledges,
pretending to be stones.
Voyeuristic stars. Hyperbolic stars.
Stars that melt on your tongue.
Stars that become planets by killing something beautiful.
A boy like you once told me how
I was up all last night, dying.
The moon stepped from her shoes, stepped off the ledge;
she landed in the front yard,
her dress over her head and her legs pulling hard
toward the center of the earth.
I'm sure I heard the stars cheering for her death,
their voices like opening up a skull,
like light when it comes inside you, for the first time,
the heat, the subjective parts of your body
under siege, and I know I heard the waves
whispering to the beach, dilettante heartbreakers each.
Words *are* enough, bet me.
The trees, the grass, the cars in the drive, the stars.
I started this letter fifteen times.

The stars bending down to kiss you,
to tear off your face if you have one.
You have one, you don't have one, the stars bending down to kiss you.
They will find the right moment to hurt you, which is love,
which is stars, who are coming.
Sing to them by stepping from your shoes.
Call to them; promise them the world.
I'll hide behind the corpse of the moon
and when they reach for you, I'll hold them down
while you do the worst thing you think of.

Zombie Sunday (The Dear Reader Version)

Gentle handed holy father, or whomever,
        must we both stay as far and beautiful
as we are tonight? You are the land
        and now it looks as if I'm going to land
somewhere in the ocean off you.
        Lately, I miss the orchestrated
feasibilities of earth. Down there
        (call it Nebraska) they read from left
to right, like *Hamlet*, and even the tires
        smell like spikenard, so maybe
I'll make it, partially Germanic, weightless
        above the plains, reconfiguring
my window, zeroing in on the whatsit.
        And like the astronaut I am always
of two minds about re-entry, but you are not
        coming for me, there are no rescue
helicopters, no more sins beyond fruit
        and—*Gott in himmel*—zee decolletage,
and I hear you whispering, just off screen,
        like a silent film director, feeding
your scale-wage children the expressions
        guaranteed to make me flinch.
Zee world is lousy with zee extras.
        Zey are so shapeless, like zee bear.
It is so difficult, GHHF, to reconcile the stars
        with my day to day ebullience.
Perpend: I puked mint julep
        on the badminton court.
Apparently, I contain universes,
        ill-born, constellatory pin-points
thusly supernovaed into grass.
        I saw you reaching for your high-lighter
like a samurai. Like a samurai
        I've got something for you
to explicate. What further strings
        must I pull to force you
to blast me from the local ether?
        You aren't good for me,
and still, I have redistributed myself,
        according to the charts:

A) For Lent, I bollixed up my homeostasis.
         2) For you I blethered numinous
through reeds beneath a soft-core moon,
              me vaselined for the channel swim
(thank you) and footnoting beetle-trails
              with penmanship only a father could love.
C) I will re-enter the natural world.
         D) The world needs more light;
your atmosphere is thick,
              is gloomy, and I am well aware
that there are plates in restaurants
              with designs on the edges, that there
are miracles in the stream bed
              which make grown men blush,
that there is such a thing as *cornflower blue*.
         Also, I have these childhood
memories, crucified, esemplastic jellyfish
              sizzling against light-bulbs, or so
I have called them. Have taken
              to calling them. Yon blithe
teutonic heritages—skullduggery,
              bonhomie, illegitimate, all—and I promise
to allow these several objects
              their abhorrent and fetishistic
importance, if it so please you,
              though the spell-checker, whistling
like a bleached seal, has turned
              my *esemplastic* into *eczema*—have
your own sweet way, oh lord!—
              and 5) I wish I had a plywood
cut-out of your body in the giant
              mouse suit—minus the head—so I
could pose behind it, get my picture
              taken, put it on the book-jacket.
You made the amusement park
              taste like peaches. I'll never be able
to trust you with the roller coaster now.

War Poem

My platoon is all gung-ho
about defilading and amassing,
about Bob Hope and Sun Tzu,
and yet we never met a rat-fuck wog
we didn't like. Right now they're creeping
toward us, through the mist,
like pilgrims. Often we are tearful

when we deliver them
with our incredible weaponry,
and when they cry it sounds
like chandeliers, crashing through
the trees. We're at the fingertips
of so much force; it makes us
feel like singing. They have

such trees here! With their bark
peeled back, naked, they look
like sunbathers, cooking
in the heat. They would make
lovely fenceposts. Of course
I'm also talking about the enemy,
with their upturned faces and

the creaky, handmade bandoliers
which do not match their boots.
Because I notice such things
I've often thought I should've been
a priest, and my sister says that I
am too soft to be a soldier, that I
am capable of making love with harlots

on the flag. True, I enlisted for
the hair-cut, but I was simple, my body
accounted for, and when at last
I killed them in the trees and heard
their language, I was no longer afraid
since each word could mean anything,
could exit bigger than it entered me
and blossom out like milk.

Poem to Line My Casket with, Ramona

Come practice your whorish gestures in the graveyard, Ramona.
Come sharpen your teeth on the tombstones.
Cough up the roots if you know what's good for you.
When coyotes are teaching their young to howl,
ghoulies rehearse the Courtship of Wrist-bones.
When you hear clawing at the square of styrofoam
serving as a window in the caretaker's shack,
then you must count each step going up to the mausoleum,
and my ghost will appear in the churchyard.
He'll kiss the back of your knee in the moonlight.
These are not promises, but eerie enough, regardless.
You must count out loud, Ramona, the steps,
because this is the time to watch what eats you.
I used to love the way the wind whistled through your teeth
when you drove the back roads, above your legal limit.
I used to have these poses. They turned into habits.
I used to love the folks that loved me.
And they've been sad ones, my years since being dead.
And they've been coming, the folks who claim to love me.
And I hardly recognize myself. There aren't mirrors, as such.
The drum section rattles it out, down by the high school.
I hear them, or is it the caretaker drunk in his wheelbarrow?
You used to play the wheelbarrow, I recall.
You used to wash your underwear in the sink.
Above ground, the wind whistles through the tombstones.
Below ground, the wind sleeps and has colors.
Below ground, colors are how I dream of making my comeback.
There's a difference between *a* white dress and *the* white dress.
You used to strip off *the* white dress in a highly professional manner.
You used to dangle the remote, and I'd come get it.
You used to skip church. You used to skip dinner parties.
Now you've been seen hoisting condoms from the pharmacy.
There are twelve condoms to a pack. A pack of lovers mills outside your door.
A pack of the dead are heading toward the showers.
A pack of dead lovers is referred to as "a creep" of dead lovers.
More than one dead lover is weeping. But oh, how it was me who loved you then.
You with your cracked lips, with your love and your other defilements kept alive
       in a bucket.
When I first died, I stole a lock of your hair while you slept.
Now I dip it in ink when the mood strikes,
and the times you visit and kneel so pretty on the grass above me,
that's not scratching you hear. It's writing.

Zombie Sunday (The Epic Version)

Gentle handed holy father, or whomever,
please hum a few bars of the song

I'm supposed to sing, and have forgotten,
that human song which calls the dejected

home from the heat of the compost heap
where I spend my lonely winters

as the Visiting Minister of Seeds,
where the slugs roll like seals in my lungs

and I'm lit through the mouth like an opera
by these extra holes in my skull

which exhale, now, in addition to your usual
and holy golden light, a medicinal fog

that attracts the talented beetles—
whom I'd like to thank for all their efforts—

who crawl for miles to stroke my tongue
and scrape their wings across my teeth,

hence giving me this lovely bit of voice, this little breath
to make up stories for the melon rinds

or tell you where it hurts the least.

The Horse Leech's Daughter

The horse leech's daughter is a closed system.

—Samuel Beckett

From a coffin hinge you've made yourself
a wedding ring, and I hear you can't get to sleep these days

without perfuming your bathroom mirror
on the spot where the reflection of your white neck

rises each morning, like an intestine,
as if even your glassed-up jugular could pump

the required lavender heat to send the stable hands
running to you with your daddy's leather

satchel, packed with the good daughter's cure.
Don't you think I saw the pair of coveralls

in your closet, above the fingerprint kit,
below the formaldehyde jar, beside your ether-

soaked rags, the day I left? And here, I am king
of all I survey—a teapot, the ocean down the street,

and one hundred oblong egg-casings spacing
the beach: the water's insectile come-ons, bereft of hope and slime.

This is my first chapter on home forensics,
and this is my new girlfriend, Sea-Bass.

Look at her dress, so rough and slippery.
And look, my time has come, my name on the next superfetatory convulsion

of the earth, on into a fresh, libertine nexus,
a crease in one of god's little footprints,

but there are so many names mouldering
in the bone-yard, without bodies to inhabit.

Like the peg-legged dog of an old crypt-raider
I will fetch you a new name like a bone

from the dirt, when your time comes,
and I will fetch you your slippers and your pipe, when the time comes.

Some days I watch the ocean down the street,
and it's like with a tongue that the water cuts

the sand into ribbed shelves, and it's like with love
that the tongue drools on the taut, brown stomach

of the beach, and it's like the tide that I invent
a thing to love, then cover it with water.

Zombie Sunday (Had We but World Enough and Time)

Gentle handed holy father, or whomever,
how I love curling up on the moldy couch
in the vacant lot, across from the skating rink,
where I pretend to hold your hand, in the rain,
and we are queer for each other, are we not?
You've dropped, like a lady's handkerchief, your several hints:
the bible, for example, which was a gift,
and where you wrote on the inside cover—
like a green school girl—your first name with my last.
Also the flowers, who offer their meager,
vegetable kindness when you are lonely for my voice.
Yet this is no time for the trademark
coyness, when matter is decaying,
when the stars, don't think I haven't noticed,
are stuck in clots and barely sparking,
like bad plugs, and the celestial spheres
have ground to a missionary halt.
GHHF, or whomever, you are old enough
to be my mother, or whatever,
and all the old girlfriends are jealous.
You have drowned one world already,
so confident, so tall, yet when lightning flashes,
I have to think, it is your knees that crack.
Baby, what are you waiting for?
I see how you look at me, across rooms,
like I'm just the kind of firmament
you could really cast some light onto,
and with those knees, like two greased moons
in glass sacks, if you fell to them,
and asked, how could I say no?
The very rivers would double back
to their invisible mothers and the mountains
would cross their legs and squirm.
So loose the bald hinges of the universe
and step down through the canopy.
Come over here and tell me who you like.
Come sit in the back row during Algebra class
and let's see the skin that time forgot,
let's do the math, let's knock the handle
off the moon, let's review the tape,

let's practice your lines, and lord when you left me
I turned in my library card, I shaved
my head and wept for days, the sun
pulsing like a tumor in a bank of cloud
above the pawn shop, inoperable and shy.
Who but me will take you in?
You, who could clean us from the very streets—
between your holy thumb and forefinger—
like so much scum on floss? You have
stricken me, thusly, there-over, from the records
even once. But now I'm going to have
to have those inimitable favors of yours,
a peek across the sizable dowry of time,
and as sordid and easy as you were
in the days of old, with your debutante
sea-splitting and the profligate haunting
of the hedge, if you do come again,
come eagerly, like it was your first time,
and please have the nerve to wear
something abominable and white.

Poem Voted Most Likely

To refer to your heart as *The Penguinery*
To bronze your heart-shaped knees
To run numbers up the flagpole
To vespertine Sophia
To chia-pet the fairway and to shrinky-dink the admiral
To love your colorized body even more than the original
To knit cob-webs out of sugar cubes while the fulsome, diegetic mergatroid
        of space and time collapses
To drown in a library
To contain imaginary toads with real cherry bombs in them
To marry someone "special"
To deliver a papal bull to a Jagermeister girl
To bounce a check for veggie bacon at the local food co-op
To depants Maude Gonne or raffle off a politician, pick one
To drink its hot-dog water like a good fellow
To laminate the small of your back
To act as interim liaison to the Psychedelic Mole People
To huff on tractor fumes
To throw you in the casino pond when you've set yourself on fire
To bootleg moonshine in a tuba
To smoke that ass
To come around for a second pass over Kankakee, at midnight
To sew itself inside a patient
To be epicene in doorways
To page you at the ballet
To show your boyfriend something nifty, over by the pie-safe
To define "mortician's dozen"
To age from 18 with a bullet straight to 40 at the buffet
To haul you to the Cineplex for the matinee interrogation
To watch your lips move while you read
To breathe when you breathe, sweet-pea

Zombie Sunday

Gentle handed holy father, or whomever,
tonight I only sent one invitation, so am relieved

when I arrive, bulling in post-verbal
off the crowded street, no more bowing down

before the goblin-lidded traffic lights,
my brain exploding like a pheasant

from my head at last, bursting harried
from the tree-line at your foot-fall

and whirring through the air, disconnected
from the messages you have left

for it on earth, game-bird, the bar food shiny, the rail tequila
aquavivid napthalene, and here

you are again, you're following me,
once that blind balloon man

who slipped a naugahyde bible
in my pocket as I slunk past,

once that heartless bartender
who gave my drink to another man,

but this time a woman, cast
in your weekend image, her reflection cast

off the bar mirror, my skull a cast
and it itches underneath, if I could just

slip the chopsticks right inside and scratch,
fetch the haywire nodal cabbage out

and snap it like a wrinkled towel
and fold it into something intricate,

an origami terry cloth crane, a crispy lotus
unperturbed, then might I gather up the strength

to tell you what I really think, which is a sentence
that starts convincingly with *Stitch*

and ends up lost in Tuscaloosa, land
of subject, where all used sentences come

to drown each other out, and Night will have its porter house
schadenfreude rare, so drink quick baby,

they don't serve your kind in here,
big *G* gods with their superstructures

all carefree and ballistic, your hair *adagio*
(you are so small—you are a teleology),

and lo your mattress, true, the gamesome horse
which pulls this sentence through the park, O park,

O little GHHF—your mattress
tres fascistic-palomino-something-charger—

you are a need and nothing other, a guilty
midnight yearning for the reverse

cow-girl, the morning cigarette
lit wrong-ways at the filter, the illiterate

tumblerful of scotch a crystal kindergarten
in your continental hand,

and in this bar your face, her face,
the *same* face—get me?—and that same face

the face which is the club that drove
this sentence to the green, O green,

O in the shadow of such a face
in such a bar on such a night the days

live briefly, like houseflies, like those good ideas
you sent which slip away, in turn, like days

if I don't write them down, your face, her face, the negotiable
flame retardant mask the kids all want

for Halloween, and your hand, too,
the means to diagram the declarative

sentence of my death, no assembly required
and likewise all the rage this year.

Love Double-Wide (Your Love Is Like a Bad Tattoo)

Your love is like a bad tattoo.
I've done too much time
in this trailer park and I will
burn your double-wide down

except I'm lazy. Your love
is like a bad tattoo although
you put it on the back of my
eye. It starts "Ramona" and I

can't read the rest anymore.
I'm tired but I remember what
it says. Something I won't
repeat is what. I said "love"

but meant a word that sounds
like "trigger" and means
"You're dead." Look it up
if you don't believe me.

Find it near "damn fool"
and "dear god" if there ever
was such a dictionary. And if
there was, you sure already

read it. I studied some Latin
strictly due to you: *Semper
fidelis, semper idem, semper
paratus.* Always faithful,

ready, and the same. Me or you,
what a question. Anymore
I'm like some Ophelia who took
the other route, fat, drugged,

and gone to seed. Alive though.
Lounging in the wading pool
outside fair Hamlette's double-wide
in my best plastic sunglasses

and checking my periphery as if
epiphanies might have to sneak
right up on the likes of me. I'm in
need of some coy flowers, a cocktail.

Somebody bring my notebook, too.
I'll write one of my patented I didn't
kill myself notes: *Hello cruel world
I'm still not leaving again, it's me.*

Your love is like a bad tattoo
deep on my superstructure.
What monks scribble on bones
in ossuaries, I imagine. My latest

affectation is pretending you are
a house I'm haunting with my life.
You don't think I'm pretending.
Somebody bring me my hood.

Pantoum for Houston (Director's Cut)

Well here we are in love again & don't you fly
& hide your pretty face from me, Houston.
I haven't had hands in thirteen years.
When I had hands, there was a pink planet hidden

inside a pretty face, Houston, a pink pill
stuck in the throat. It was so hard to get it down.
When I had hands there was a pink planet hidden
& sad stories of how I lost my hands, pink

& stuck in the throat, so very hard to get them down.
Lt. Jackson reads my private mail, sad letters
w/theories on what happened to my hands.
She hunts archaebacteria w/tiny sharpened words

& secretly she reads my private mail, although—
it must be said—she also writes my private mail.
She hunts archaebacteria w/tiny sharpened words
or chews the air so I can breathe, & like I said—

must it be said?—she also writes my private mail,
ie, *please save your spit in a jar or I will milk you*
& then she chews the air to paste so I can breathe
& asks me *where's the scalpel, please?* or *music please?*

or *please save your spit in a jar or I will milk you*
like a viper. I've read everything Jupiter published.
Where's the scalpel when the music in me
is a giant spider? Swallow me gently, Houston,

like a viper. I've read everything Jupiter published
& I don't think Jackson's much of an actress, her
or the giant spider. Swallow me, Houston, gently
feed me my lines, my pink hands are missing

& I don't think I'm much of an actress. I haven't
had hands in thirteen years. Feed my lines
to Lt. Jackson & use my hands to mime the story
of Here We Are In Love Again & Don't You Fly.

Sheriff, You Forgot Yer Hat

Ramona, I can't sleep, I shot
too many Indians. I shot and shot
but they wouldn't fall down. Such as it was
I reached for the sky. I selected
my cactus of the hour. I recollected
fanciful things. Late frost last year
I watched you pull your long-johns
stiff and frozen off the clothesline
like a flag. Did I remove my hat?
There are whole days I'm ashamed of,
and riding no-handed through the saloon
I often think of them. Soon I'll write
a letter to you, describing all of this.
When I reach for my pencil, it will be there.

Milk Division

I duct-tape a border down the middle
of every room—my side, your side—
so I won't be able to watch the clock
and you won't be able to see the mirror
while you dress each morning, and I'll
have to lean across the plants to tell you
what shoes you're wearing with what hat.
It's a good system. If your toes wander
onto my side of the bed, I'll keep them
and raise them as my own, and one day
you'll come home early and you'll catch me
with your half of the milk. This is all
in the future. Goddamn, you'll say,
we should have tried this years ago.

In My Oft-Quoted *Guide to Clouds and Weather*, Ramona

In my oft-quoted *Guide to Clouds and Weather*, Ramona, the fog terrifies itself.

Contrails blossom into storm fronts, and even the skywriting, under your covers, gets
    me reaching for the umbrella.

In the weather's words it's hard to say what I'm so never like.

Dark clouds pop out of your eyes.

I haven't even gotten to the heavy systems.

This morning, you awaken with a fever. Yesterday, it was mine.

Now, we are finally on page 10, where I am so happy to have infected you.

Most clouds are made from glitter and the juice you squeeze from cannonballs and force
    your enemies to drink.

These dark ones come from your eyes.

But the personality hand on the clock in your heart sweeps toward a cloudless day in May,
    so it says, right here, in my oft-quoted
        Guide to Clouds and Weather,
        have a look.

Find it above, "The more sympathetic mountains gather hoods about their heads, and cry."

But here you are, Hurricane What's-Your-Name, about as beautiful as you are
    willing to tear a hole in my chest.

Also, the lenticular altocumuli look quite lovely tonight, reflected by your teeth.

The way I tell a storm is coming is, there's this stranger making love to herself,
    next door, a woman I don't care about,
        and then my hands turn into
          anemone.

That's when I know to touch you.

And the moon, who has a little to do with the weather, likes to see the kid with the
anemone for hands, so she lets me take control
of the tides for awhile.

I take the ocean for a ride through the hallway, through the walls, through your teeth,
then through with me.

That's when I know a storm is coming.

Me, I like to have control. Ask the cirrus clouds in the stratosphere, on page 37,
the anemic clouds that forewarn
thunderstorms.

I get a call from an old friend, then comes the tsunami in the carpet.

You step out for a late beer, then the ocean at our doorstep.

You know how to play hell with the littoral zones.

In the past, I've labeled it Seasonal Affection Disorder, but the symptoms keep changing.

The rules are always different, nothing gloams in the moronic twilight, but then a web
of lovely green mist, in the kitchen.

Reach out for that rain, it counsels you an acrobat's posture.

Which is something-or-other *saltatoris*, in Latin, in the scientific glossary of my oft-quoted
Guide to Clouds and Weather.

And you ask, "How is the sky so pretty, and blue?"

Despite what we both know, and the tornado, there's nothing inexplicable
beneath the bed.

The sky is a heavy blue eel held up between you and where you're headed.

A theme park of weather-related maladies.

A white tongue caught in a black umbrella.

Surviving Love

Remember my best night?
I thought I did. Always in your light.
The cold rain, porous and glycerin.
Don't talk to me about the rain or
what inconsequential oblivion awaits,
what infirm clock watching angels spill
dark-wise from tiny cars like clowns.
A plastic thermometer in my chest
pops and tells me that we're done.
Breakfast then comes pouring in
with the new shadows, and coffee.
Clouds approach. Lies flood
the bad neighborhoods of my tongue.
You move to turn on the light
and it's some time before it lights.
Hello, hello. Hello? Your navel
proves to me that you were born.
That living things die in false ones.
Remember me, like a mouth that
opens on the dark. I'll remember you
like a grave forgets what fills it.

Zombie Sunday

Gentle handed holy father, or whomever,
they broke the mold before they made you
except on second thought you weren't

made at all, they had to drill for you, they had to pry
your fossil from the jealous rock,
they want to carbon date you, to take you

for a spin, to hold your hand
and close their eyes when you lean in
because they love you, oh they love you, your hillbilly

swagger on the mound, the unexpected
side-arm wind-up, your teeth soughing
sweetly in your mouth, an albino

field of wheat, and you tried to put the *I*
in *team*, you tried the first prayer
out of the drawer of prayers, behind

the socks, back corner, next to the lubricant, oh you tried
your best with me, but forgot to flesh
me out, and for that last important bit

of skin, I would stand up on my hind legs,
suddenly evolved, gorgeous as your
barbered trees in winter, epiphanic

as a motherfucker, and I would eat
a cross of brick, I have filled your pillowcase with bees

so I can sterilize my mouth with gin
and suck the stingers from your neck,
for I am the loathsome chalk artist

reluctantly commissioned with the side-walk
outline of your body, and you're the comeback
second-stringer, the player-to-be-named-later,

the first-person-omniscient who plagiarized
the *Autobiography of the World* and called out dibs
on the future flower box my skull.

Sleeping with Waitresses

And I have this pitcher of wretched coffee,
but my waitress doesn't care that I love her
now or whenever I've come stumbling in,
when sleep (it's said) is a figure skater
skating tight white figures across 4am
and the pillows knock like old boxcars
and bald God's own true daylight flirts

creepily on the young knee of the day.
Now some new terror in the sugar bowl.
I'd sleep beneath the eggs, as it were.
I'd frame the house of toast with sausage.
I'd lock out heaven from its dripping
door, pull the pancakes to my chin,
sigh, and make my waitress come in

and get me. Come in, I'd say, and get me.
Please sleep with me if that means sleep.
Later, we'll have our way with the special.
Your knees look cute from this angle.
I say cute, but they make me cry.
My napkin isn't warm enough and I
am in love with how you think I don't

exist, in love with your sweet disdain and
the what looks like it must be a mustard stain
on your sleeve, Cindy. Stay until the walls
get cold. Kiss the furniture from my lips.
Tell me a story that ends with *It was all
a dream*. I'll tell you one that begins
with a mattress swinging on a meat-hook.

Meditation on Insomnia

Kung-Fu, a couch, and I might reach
emptiness tonight, stuck on that Midwest
hoo-doo, counting cemetery steps
to a hundred in my head. The television,
that affable poltergeist, will pull me
through. That's what they should mean
when they call it a tube—the tunnel that vision
becomes. Cross-haired and blue. Priceless,
mon cheri, my blessing from a god
thought to be in hiatus, a panderer
between insomniac and dizzy-lashed
sleep. But soft, on screen, she's a walking
stick and a ballerina clown, a glove of liquid
marble clinging to golden kindling.
In this, her latest martial arts affair,
Michelle Yeoh decimates her black-clad
opposition effortlessly, operating
within the impeccable timing of sleep.
It's said the attraction of Hong-Kong
action flicks lies in the fact that no one
acts; the fear is real. Michelle's legs
are too short to stop the motorcycle
after her jump to the roof of the speeding
train, and so she dives from it—the
train, the motorcycle. I don't care
that the fear is real. I've burned a green
candle down to a bowl shaped lump.
As I pass my hand over the flame,
and back, I put a flicker in the light.
I know I read lips because this dubbing
blinds my comprehension—the volume's
too low. Nicely, the shape of her mouth,
and what she says, collide. I, too, have
done my own stunts. At times like this
the need for sleep becomes emotion,
and Michelle, after running as long as she can
from certain death, turns, lets her body
fill empty spaces, enforces herself. Once,
I read that Michelle Yeoh nearly died
on the set of a movie about a stunt-woman

who died on set, one of those layered,
mythical moments when what's been
called Time stops, and it's alright to kill
yourself. There was a blind spot. Michelle
was to jump thirty feet into the bed
of a moving truck with nothing but her
director's word that the truck would fill
the required space. Sometimes, it's hard
to lie heart-side down on the bed. Often,
I don't trust my lungs to fill by themselves
and the blood pressure rises in my ears
until it crunches like footsteps in old snow.
Michelle's real name is Yeoh Choo Kheng.
She danced ballet at four. If I had a straw
I'd suck wax into my mouth, let it pool,
take shape. As tired as I am, who knows
when they'd find me, sleeping with a replica
of empty space on my tongue. After a while,
sleep comes so hard and fast you can feel
like you are falling. Everybody knows that.

Drugstore

I finished the baggie of blue pills
that made the planets so tolerable.
The toy hula girl on top of my dresser

sends her regards, although she
doesn't dance until I touch her,

and Ramona, do you have any new pills
you're not using, any spare lows

for your only boy? I fell hard
for the mailbox, I sent flowers to

that mailbox, I went fishing
in the reservoir, but they'd drained it

twenty feet. Your lost lures glared
cheaply under the morning sun,

which was a plug in a reprobate
bathtub. Will we drain up

instead of down? If we go down
is that the first we're heard of?

Yes. I'm tired of the astrologies,
the icy pharmaceutical rites

that are enough for me. I grow old.
I encounter philosophy at night.

I'm concerned that what we have
is each other, for as long
as prescribed, and I can tell

by the skin beneath your eyes
that as far as I go, it's your word
against the universe and sleep.

Zombie Sunday

Gentle handed holy father, or whomever,

    the stars swing in like buccaneers

        through the windows, and they are

beautiful, and they are yours, of course,

    ditto cherry tree, and wildebeest—

        how many times must you remind me?—

and I am searching, now, for the French phrase

    for albino field of wheat. O mon pere etc

        doux ouvrier sacre, your white teeth

are learnéd. They read much of the night,

    they go South in Winter, they ripple loosely

        along the pale gum-line like those spirits

on the haunted shore, which have elsewhere

    been compared to leaves, but are really

        more akin to grease, also rippling

loosely. Oh asphodel! that something

    flower. Oh but we should be able

        to walk said shore and name the genus

and the species. O GHHF, your coffee beans

    meant nothing. They kept me on the phone

        all night. I am a burnt arrow now, loosed

from the Anglo Saxon bow your body.

You dream like a battleship turns.

Your two hands blooming folded,

from a black vase, was an image

I thought up, once, to help get me to sleep.

Oh but the sleep I lost, considering your sleep.

And I am mostly sure that loss is French

(*le* terror-dome) and will follow me

as far as Pittsburgh, human sacrifice or no, but I know

for sure that loss transforms the delta, and is also how

you change your mind. Even now

the Mississippi bends to your fuzzy will

and carves toward Jerusalem. I am the paraclete of loss

in the House of Catalepsis. I am bald

as the wind. Or was it lorikeet, like Matthew said?

Matthew, patron saint of the poult-footed and the rain.

Oh GHHF, you should read him, you might

learn a thing or two about yourself.

Thirty shekels is a lot of jack, anyhow.

And I have failed your comprehensive tests before, oh lord.

I am searching, now, for the French phrase

for *lorikeet of loss*, scaly breasted and /

or blue-fronted rainbow, *Trichoglossus chlorolepidotus*

and *Charmosyna toxopei*, respectively.

I pilot the cuttlefish and tree the seeds.

I will burn the very Latin from the world.

I weep for every cheating drink

I have forgotten, that hooligan wine

in Cerbere, for example, who loved the carpet

so well, so much more than it loved me,

and I am circling over this your every sentence

as you drive it, looking for the loophole,

but you will evade me in the driveway,

you will leave me for the rumored

carpet, you will ditch me cold forever

on the airless, sunspot runway where our bodies

made more sense. They called me

the hyacinth girl. The ocean was my stepsister,

pregnant with a style of fish you dreamed

last autumn, but in any language I am Isadora,

zombie queen of the Appalachians.

I knelt beside you yesterday.

I bet you prayed for rain.

Sleeping with J.A.

Here sleeps the book I have swatted bees with,
the book dropped down three flights of stairs,
the book I propped on the doorknob
above a bucket of broken glass to warn me
when the intruders come, when it's time
to forgo books, and when my imagination
is that suspicious delivery van hunched
across the street, with no bouquets in back,
this is the book that sleeps with me.
John Ashbery, your Book of selected poems

is a slut with nickels for teeth, and a chin!
I love it, and the poems are a different story.
They are a semi with soft brakes and a Honda
in front of it, who is me. Sometimes, what the
hell are you talking about? I get the feeling
when I read them obsessively and often
that I'm not as good as I should be as
a person. I feel like taking Adult Education
classes, like Home Ec. or wood shop, something

with computers. So I could learn to get away
with things. How do you get away with
things? Yesterday I found myself quoting one
particularly exhausting turn in your big
poem about Parmigianino. I get the feeling
if I could see that painting it wouldn't
make a difference. Therefore, I do not
go to the library today and get a book
about him (Francesco). You have hamstrung
my unusually strong will to better myself,

which is why I love your book! It is and not
your fault. Better people than me tell me about
how you're a genius. I eat lunch gladly
with them, and hear serious things. I believe.
And yet at night with the ridiculous clock
I slide your book beneath the pillows
and turn toward the television, supreme
in my knowledge that what I don't know
won't hurt me, that what John Ashbery knows

I'll sleep blue shapes right through,
and maybe I should quit now, but I've been
dreaming John Ashbery again! Dogs are barking?
How I love courting the literati! But John,
get serious now. In my mind, a decapitated monkey
spins clockwise. The surveillance camera picks up
the murderer hiding in the bathroom. John,
this is how I've used my superiors, by witnessing
things I do not trust, by making love I don't
know the angles for, by identifying with animals,

by cataloguing worthwhile information, by
watching ten stupid worlds outside my window
and then looking at your poems to see
if any of it came true. That monkey's head
looks up to see if he knew what was good
for him. Mornings, I don't usually wake up
and check under the pillow to see what pages
I marked. If you only broke my head open,
this second, candy would come spilling out.

First, Second, Twenty-Fifth, and Thirty-Ninth Lines Courtesy of Thomas Campion

There is a garden in her face.
There is a garden in her face
which she carries on her head.
There is a garden on her head

which is connected to her neck,
which is a root, and there is much
rendering forth in Fall, when you
can shake her by the trunk and catch

the heavy fruit that tumbles
from her mouth, provided, of course,
that you can find the apple tree
growing somewhere in the garden

on her head. If that's a garden
on her head, then I'm reaching
for her eyes. I stalk her like
a migrant worker. I wear a mask

and walk the tiny rows. She exhales
pesticide. The squirrels die. I
position the obligatory stone
gnomes, the cheap birdbath.

I tell her there are starving kids
in China who would kill to suck
on her pomegranate forehead.
I tell her she could feed the world.

There is a garden in her face.
There are baskets in the shed.
I'm not into sharecropping
and there is something awfully

mobile about this garden.
It will come inside the house
for a glass of water if it needs one.
Or up the steps and to the bedroom.

Now a garden in the bedroom.
A garden walking into doors.
A mouthy cantaloupe who cleans
its teeth with monofilament.

All that witchy photosynthesis
and each morning an inch taller.
There is a garden in her face.
I am just about to touch it.

And I have always dreamed
of feeding a garden to itself,
of redefining husbandry.
Now a garden in the kitchen.

Toads in the furrows. Insects
in the weeds. Sometimes
the seeds spit out her name
when she spits out the seeds.

Poem against Matt Guenette's Ex-Girlfriend

Cape of Flies, memory manufactured
in Hong Kong, you have turned over
a new bridge, and you have burned
the leaves, and I think I met you once
in Carbondale, when I drove in from Iowa
to watch Matthew read the poem
of the famous chihuahua's nuts, and after
the reading, back at Matt's, Matt
brought out the picture of his brother,
drunk at a party in Ames, waving
his cock like a wand amid mixed
and unsuspecting company, as if, thus
and presto, he'd turn them all to frogs,
and I recall a woman in that picture,
off to one side, looking calmly down
at the sudden penis with a jeweler's
studied eye. Though it was not you
I remember you as that pictured girl,
caught acquisitive, hands on hips, eyes
locked in and pupils superfluous
with light. Then I moved to Virginia Beach
to teach and write, and a couple
months later, walking beneath the bridge,
I knelt to pick up a snarled bikini top
and when I pulled it from the sand
I heard a click, and found myself
caught as backdrop in a picture, just taken,
of a Navy man and wife. I imagine
them now, the Navy man back from duty,
the two of them safely couched
and sifting through vacation photographs,
their happy faces turning strange
to see me crouching on the beach
behind them, throwback avatar looking straight
past the camera, hoarding the empty cloth
as if it were the shed template of God
or further proof against the sun,
and next morning, Matt sent me the poems
in which you first appeared, beautiful
and burning at various stakes, sweet

and lovely right down to your bubbling
candy heart. I did not know you then, and I do
not know you now, Matt's ex-girlfriend,
abstract, laminated bronze snuff film
shooting nightly, behind schedule,
in the crowded hook and shiv factory
where memory is housed. Two days later
I would run up that treacherous beach,
my right hand on fire, a fluke sting-ray
tail-spike buried in my palm, and that night,
drunk enough to take out my own
cock in public, the puncture wound
on my palm a third-string irony
at best, I wrestled my bedroom
door off its hinges, walked it down
to the beach, and spoke of domesticity
beguiled. Would you believe me
if I told you I met a woman that night
who reminded me of you, who walked up
blond and resonant during my back-
assward sermon in the dunes? I didn't.
It was me and the cat-shit and the ghost
crabs, my sick hand fat and yellow
as a life raft, and three years have passed,
and you have labored under different
names, but sometimes, say if I've been
working all night, my fingers
will stiffen and curl, and I can feel the rough
black muscle of that antique fish
still twitching in my wrist, dictating
the vague, submarine compositions
of pilchard oil and trash, and I can
shut my eyes and see Virginia Beach,
the epileptic coast pole-axed
by an acetone surf, the sun-block
sealing off each body from the next,
and memory the air-tight junk fish
poking like a stylized font from the sand.

The Care and Feeding of Mermaids

Far from Indiana and the soup we made of her bones
lies the ocean, cheap and full of secrets.
There are certain things you have to know.
We carried her over land, iced down in a truck.
We remember her eyes, mostly, orphaned
and crossed by the sea. We fed her
bits of herself, and other fish.
We checked and rechecked the math.
We stuck her with vitamins, wrapped her in wet cloth.
Otherwise, we believed, her legs would begin,
but the fever that would have killed her anyway
had made the skin tough above the flesh,
a sheet of rusting steel across a soft bed,
and there was the smell of ammonia.
Her heart was dying, and protective of rain, which was her blood,
which is one thing the books were wrong about, make note.
It's true that most of the myth
we'd already murdered by the shore
when we drew her from the net,
and when our palms burned into the slime that gilded her
it smelled of apricots cooked in mud.
We looked and looked for the gills.
Starfish called from the waves
with a sound one could have mistaken for laughter,
but most of us heard as instructions.
The gulls seemed to drop from webs
out of a sky impossible to read.
How to feed her air was a concern, but briefly.
Someone cried out about lungs
and wrapped her hair with kelp.
Yes, she flopped, but as a woman would.
I went to the gas station for ice and bait,
but mostly she was lost from the start.
Later, when we separated the top from the bottom,
I couldn't help but think
we were seeing the last of something.
We found pills and bread inside her, you should note.
We saved samples of tissue,
pale wafers of information which give us hope.
But there was no tool, no matter how sharp,

could dissociate her eyes,
could find the difference between the foam and dirt
in her biology, not there.
We knew enough not to try
until we were full and sad, like cartridges.
At first the eyes seemed healthy on their own,
freed, come-hither, and looking West for the body
which we'd dumped in a ditch, lord help us.
It is in this way that surgery helps you think, like what we did with her legs
(I see them still, electric and pink),
though I do not wonder what she thought of us,
brave and ashen, embarrassed for our hands.
She didn't have a language to tell us anyway;
just ragged whispers toward the end,
like a god being forced through a keyhole.
Some men who heard her dove into the rocks.
Those who did not die wonder of their pulses, to this day,
and search for it in their wrists.
So the throat and tongue we fear to examine,
though we've preserved them, and they fail to sing.
One hopes she thought well of us, however,
when we finally did the quiet thing
then laid her on the table. Her eyes
were lonely for nerve and reef;
the night was young; two plus two
was often four, and all across America
beauty comes to such an end.

Space Dementia

She was older than I thought,
but who, looking out on the long
unsolved coming future of language,
could have described her, held her
to the light like an x-ray and found
the shadow that could betray her?
Her passport. The Café des Artistes.
Eastern Europe. Prague specifically.
I was not that shadow that could.
It was one of those meetings with
a codename on the lips and a romantic,
simple hate of foreign countries.
Heavy eyeshadow, a shadow, a finger.
I could not even touch her then,
absinthe burning in my eye which
was the eye of God. They say (I said)
Persius' Aunt wrote the book on
tasteful civic suicide, cried out,
"Look! How simple!" It's all simple
when you're sure to die, I told her.
Perhaps you have a plastic leg, your
right breast drips sweat. Hell.
You'll hug his neck. It's all simple.
I was younger than I thought. She
advised me not to hold my breath.
I could hardly look at her then.
I could not hope to leave or fly.
She spoke of a church in Naples
where angels absconded to Mexico
with the working props of the nave.
Oh, and they *never* came back.
Since this is the place we've found
ourselves in, (she said) who knows
where we've turned up missing
or where they pray for us to be.
So, raise your glass. God give us
strength to learn the uses of these
tools we've broken, that we might
find our way. I didn't drink with her
and I didn't travel space. The city
made this face, like a whore surprised
she's coming. Half liquor, half mother.

Epithalamion, Ex Post Facto

I.

Ramona you went ahead and married
the tannest Christian bank machine
in Illinois. For thirty years his infant lips
have cycled toward you, like an escalator

across his tiled face. Where was my invitation?
What poem was I writing? Every bride
is gartered for a reason. Every bride
is a lonesome holocaust, contains

secret prophecies she whispers
only to the buffet table. When I heard
you arced the bouquet a little high
and it went to sudden potpourri

in the ceiling fan of the Lincoln Ballroom,
Holiday Inn, Riverside Drive,
I remembered that I've always been
a sucker for the thought of you

tiered and bridal, coiffed by nymphs
and right with God. But now you're belted
supine in Nassau, your honeymoon
an acheless continuation of motions

you began before I met you
when I met you in the forest, before
the thing called time. Your future bridegroom
was only kindling then, a glimmer

in your eye, and I was yet an epoch
from the thought of you together,
spread out like maps on the bathroom tile,
your incandescent wedding dress

an afterthought flung into the harbor
and riding back to the beaches
like a poisoned white tide. Swim
at your own risk, Ramona:

whoever marries now, will long
stay so: whoever reaches out
reaches out with empty hand.

II.

Ramona, come on over when you have the time, slip the *film noir* in my mouth.

Bring me your new name, on a platter.

I take thee, in the bed of my pick up truck, in sickness and in health, looking over
the tailgate to the rock quarry, your eyes on gypsum and mica, your pager
vibrating lonely on the dash.

I take thee, 17th century style, both of us in hats. I will give unto thee my two thumbnails,
eventually black.

You need something old, and I am old. You need something new, and I am new.

But I am also surgical. Accessible. Predictable. I am the oblong facsimile,
fatter in winter.

I am lozenged up in liturgy and epiclesis: I call you, learnéd sister, down from Jupiter's
craggy knee, to sing your own wedding song.

I take thee with or without your dearly belovéd, stupefied in the pews by my ridiculous
good looks.

I take thee corseted by whalebone, stoned on the halfshell, strolling down the esplanade.

And wasn't it just this Sunday last you drove me out behind the Super K and handed me
the braided rope?

Your old name shook from your body like a booster rocket. I entered its ruined consonants
in the spotless lists of time.

Now I take this abandoned name as my own. I collect it, I strap it on and belt it out
when called upon in waiting rooms and queues.

I wish you long married afternoons alone. Crisis on a Wednesday. I wish you married silence
over books, I wish you bad television, difficulties reproducing family recipes.

Some say I met you in an ambulance, New York City. You wore your "do not rescuscitate"
    heels and you smelled like iodine.

I also met you at the kindergarten dance, 1803.

Oh Hans, you pulled my pigtails, and we picked a cot and took our nap together.

We slept through bird-strike, through genocide, through crack-house and the sloughing off
    of galaxies and scientific paradigm, at all times innocent of nothing.

You are the history of the world. I cross you, here and there, like a time-line,
        important conflagrations meted out between
                the decades of your knees.

And there are other memories in which I traffic. Dante's Envelope. The Revenant. The
    Congress of the Hovering Bee.

And that weekend, housesitting in Indianapolis, when you played Medusa and tied me
        to the bedpost with your hair. Oh, you knew a few knots I didn't:
                the bastard-hitch, the chthonic double-upside slip,
                        and the loathsome and mobius
                                overhand delight.

I take thee holy, during church, seconds after lunch with in-laws, balanced in your thoughts
        or moving to conclusions like a hammer, your many children sleeping
                in the car outside, their lungs filtering out the local air
                        like terra-form machines, and turning
                                all the black cats white.

To the bridesmaids am I supposed to take this ruination, this blight?

I wish for you, instead, a thousand lovers, each face a star in a constellation plotting out
        your face, each body rising from the bathtub, clean as any ghost,
                their lithesome silhouettes nuked into the ceiling
                        above the master bed.

Bride, gymnastic reformulator of the missionary position, intuitive counterpart of time,
        you are the shadows moving on a hundred nursery walls,
                and when the raindrops fall, you point them
                        where they go.

You are the biological father of my terrible woe.

III.
If this were Chinese time, you'd be divorced by now.
You've punished all the powdered nymphs who plagiarized your vows

and I must infect myself with wedding toasts alone.
Pick up the flowers and the phone

Ramona. Drunk, I look wonderful. I smell good too.
I don't know French, and I know less you.

If torn to rags your wedding dress could bandage a platoon.
You recline like a piano. You strike me like the moon

strikes up the tide. I will invent a little wedding dance
based on the Charleston, the defibrillator, and on the second chance.

So let the bride feel as if she's just been born.
Let the band play songs only heard in porn-

ographic movies, for I have left instructions for the groom in the corner stall.
I am the mitochondria boating through the bride's cell walls,

many and divisible, clowning like drowned men, my thousand-thousand teeth
slick with kindness and disease.
Let the uninvited wedding guest bite the bride's white knees.

Let the bride toss her bouquet into the ballroom ceiling fan.
Let the bridegroom cry over the body of his best man

and let the wonky bridesmaids sing.
If you drop a quarter in the nearest priest, you get another wedding ring.

Watching Poetry Readings on Videotape in Apartment #5

It seems we are descended from a long
extinct breed of column-legged monster
much better than us, a pulmonary
caryatid with a prehensile tongue
for kissing the kinds of kisses that turn
your children's children into dust, and you
could almost park a flat bed truck inside
each honeysuckle mouth, so there should be
less to say here, but video adds ten lines
to each poem, and the woman who lives upstairs
is young and up-to-here with dresses,
and from time to time a rusty drop
of water leaks through the bathroom ceiling
from her sink into mine, a give and take
I'm unaccustomed to, like love, which is
the FBI's jurisdiction, who tell me
there is a time to weep, a time to burn
dolls, and she goes seeping through the walls
like this, I will remind you, one drop every
six minutes, cold, enthused, wrong like a child
filling out prescriptions, like a clown guerilla
squeaking in the dunes. You're not alone,
depending on the consulted dictionary.
Depending on the consulted dictionary,
if one were more inclined to romance
one might collect this water, drop by drop,
and pour it in the window-box, but there
isn't any dictionary, just two guys thumbing
guitars on the porch, abusing the chorus
of *Feel Like Makin' Love*, over and again,
until it spreads apart, and they kick it
when it's down, abandon it outside my door
with a mitten pinned to its sleeve. If one were
more adept at voodoo than one already
was, one might also use that drip-water
to boil a soup, though one wouldn't eat
such a soup in real life, particularly
with the toe of a high heeled shoe for a spoon,

which certain brands of voodoo do advise
you will remember. But I see the way
she doesn't read anything. She thinks
like a megaphone, and what music is it
makes her wish that she were swimming,
what certain gleam in the sometimes eye?
If you don't lie, you are a surface, which is
not like the surface of a lake, which lies,
but like the membranes of the inner ear,
which are to be penetrated, or blown
apart, and blown apart is how you tell
apart, which is what the leaking pipes say,
who know you can only go around
discerning skin from formica for so long,
who have confessed they are too old
to cry, but dammit, what else is there?
Often two people—let's call them people—
come together like the slotted halves
of a bayonet clutch, and thereby set
the fat world jiggling along the bare treadmill
which, before the flood, used to be the sky,
and it's not her, exactly, so much as how
I'd like to stroll into the operating room,
order a round of anesthesia for the house
and leave my patient mumbling on the table
untouched, preparing to be survived by words,
which used as tubes are pointless and stern,
but still snake, briskly, into her helpless lungs,
and look, I have a couple brand new lines
clipped to fit snug between the shoulder blades:
for example, what's a bad poem like you
doing on a Math girl like this, and friends,
do you recall that night I spent inside
the haunted villanelle, the one with three
cheers for the martyrdom of jakes and fires?
I am used to expiring in August, bored
of being home for mail, of going straight to video
through the park. Please forward all my letters
to the handsome stranger. Stuff the mail-box,
from here on in, with liquor, porn, and trash.
It's the same old story, your average person
is a heavenly body spinning God

around a web of milk, word meets word, word
falls in love, and love is another word
for how the windows leave their frames for you
and the television opens like a flower.

Ramona's Theme

We were happier in the old songs
when the pale spiders came to take us
back into the earth. My thoughts
belonged to time. Each world we passed
was older than it seemed, deceptive
in its roots, every drop of water
a dirty moon bound to dearer,
blinder seas, our foraged bodies
clean and bright, like little teeth.
What's there left to talk about now?
We've come up from the tunnels
that once belonged to mice, where
the scared worms dream of men.
Be careful with me. The night is cold,
and I can still see the deep fish
twisting through the earth like swans.

Notes for a Movie Entitled *Revenge of the Necrophiliacs*

At first, it is easier to understand
the Revenge of the Corpses,
and even, say, at the Drive-In,
where all things are excused,
one wonders what invented affliction
the necrophiliacs think
they must get even for, what ills

would bring them to solidarity
and riot. No doubt they are loners,
preferring the company
of their own thoughts, lurking
in the musty corners of houses
their mothers willed them, weeping
into lace curtains, and we must appear

so beautiful to them, living, excitable
signatures in the universal hand,
that they want to stop time
on us, pray, and return to find,
thank God, that we haven't moved
an inch, and if you took your body away
from me, and it was my body,

and if I loved you so much, or you me,
that I cursed volition and synapse,
electrical charge, speech, free will,
and still you walked away, arms
and legs to the drugstore, alive
and thinking anything you wanted,
wouldn't that be enough? And when

you die, don't people come running
for you, suddenly protective, you
with all your thoughts pouring
down dark alleyways, your lungs
emptying like trains, and how powerful
your expectations, how terribly
warm and insignificant their hands?

Sleeping with Julia Roberts

She smelled like plastic fruit and Pablo
Neruda was her favorite poet. Her thoughts,
stoked with speed and Nietzsche
and wired by Paramount, brought out
the secret patterns of the bedroom
wallpaper: shuddering valences of time,
blue daisies, a frozen horse against which
I spread my legs, and read myself

my rights. She was crazy about pasta salad.
She never called me Ace, she never lied.
It sounded like *bourgeois* when she sneezed
and each time she came into a room
where I already was, she'd click her tongue
and snap, *you're not supposed to be
in this picture, boy*, but it was me who bought
the custom made dental pick she wore

around her neck on a silver chain,
it was me who tilted back that giant head
and worked the plaque until she screamed.
I engraved messages for archaeologists
below the gum-line. I flossed up the hot,
chalky remains of a battleship lost against
the icy floes of her crenellated teeth.
Once it was her birthday. She swallowed
the room, the room slipped into her mouth

backwards, like a car reeled into a garage,
and I realized, then, that love had evolved,
and no longer should I be concerned
with God, who tossed his dice across
her stomach, who bet her museum quality
bones against his own, then timed
her record quarter mile, and when we
felt her hit his holy bloodstream like
a B-grade nightingale, it was the death

of man. On bad nights I'd find her, adding
freakish columns of numbers on the bathroom tile,
shivering, barefoot, shit-faced on mescal,
her moon in Virgo, her father's rusty, six-hole
leather punch a souvenir bulge in the front
pocket of her unzipped purple jeans. Alice,
I'd say (she made me call her Alice),
Alice, come back to bed, the worst
is over now. Your pink mitten lung is a perfect

fit tonight, and I can already feel
your prescription-dry tongue popping
like a match down my spine. This always
worked. Her scars turned into wine. I prayed
our babies would have her beautiful,
beautiful round head, the flotsam eyes,
her webbed tongue coiled in each drawbridge
mouth, and on each tongue her god-awful name.
I was in love with her when she was played
by time. No one else can say the same.

Zombie Sunday (A Short Poetical History of Spring)

Gentle handed holy father, or whomever,
I mentioned daffodils, and the crowd went wild.
I had them, briefly, nibbling from my blistered hand.
Then I called attention to the dandelions,
popping forth like sunny, tethered corks
from the busy lawn, and the crowd went
home. Lucky for me they left. Mine
was a short list of flowers beginning
with "d," and too late, skulking through the park,
did I recall the daisy, the dahlia,
too late did I invent the dog-wort
and the dwarf poppy. Modern ways.
April. Motorcycles have begun thundering
down the wet avenues like armored bees
slick with the shattered, puddled blooms
of fragrant gasoline and oil, and I've noticed,
from a distance, that in early Spring
the trees don't, all at once, jump to life
like you've read about, but gather to them
a smoky cloud of blue, like tall children
puffing on cigarettes, until, late April, they cough up
a few green leaves. That was my mistake.
Chaucer couldn't name his flowers, either,
or he could *name* them, but couldn't tell
them apart, or I missed it if he did. It was
Spring. I was involved, moaning in the hedge
and watching college kids whack golf balls
into the drive-in movie screen, which seems,
at night, across the field, like the forehead
of a giant, worried monk, bent over and tending
to his proliferating, moonlit vegetables.
Speaking of monks, I need to read
more Chaucer. Then T.S. Eliot, about
a hundred years later, wasn't he clever?
Bravo, Tom. I can barely look a lilac
directly in the stamen, a word that never seems right
no matter how I spell it, a word little more
than a word, if that, and I always guessed Eliot
a little mortuary in the sack. That, or
(your theory) he was frightened

of the shadow of his penis, rolling unbidden,
like a scuttled go-cart, across the grooved sheets.
And the hyacinths, oh the hyacinths, a flower
I'd like to take by the pistil and fling, if only I could tell one
from a hydrangea, my second flower
beginning with "h." But about old master Eliot
we both were wrong. How like me he is.
I imagine him now, sucking flowers
into the earth like a cartoon gopher,
he was a petal hoarder. I much rather
would have slept with Williams, though he did
nothing for Spring, at least in the anthologies,
our able doctor, tapping out his poems
while a lithe America undressed in the boxy
examination room across the hall.
Read Williams in a paper gown, you tell me,
and all your dreams will come to pass.
But I forgot Emily Dickinson. We all
wanted to sleep with her. She was right
about Spring, if she wrote about it, and she
had those tendencies. My new neighbor,
homeless Jack, greets Spring with a holler.
Emily would have hated him. Me, too,
though she had a thing for abomination.
But what's Emily Dickinson got to do
with the price of methedrine, Jack might
ask. Bravo, Jack. And Rilke, Jack, Rilke was an autumn.
The tree-line overtaking the movie screen
warbles. The aforementioned flowers,
all varieties, rise like European soccer fans,
and charge the field. Spring, you sent the rain
down this rented stretch of gutter-pipe
on the wretched corner of Thomas and Lafayette.
The college kids whack arc after arc
into the monk's forehead, into the tree-line,
into the onanistic wave of oncoming
flowers. I wish I could welcome these days
when the blood begins its rolling boil,
and like a chef, in my immaculate white hat,
I could use the blood to cook a meal
that would finally please you. Daylily,
digitalis, delphinium, dianthus.

Ramona Ex Machina

And forever hence be ours this chary, *wermacht* courtship, Ramona, for you are beastly castled-off
        and treasured from me, so can't (in theory) feed the roaming megafauna, but you'd
            do better than to let my open mouth
be closing now outside your jurisdiction, and even though I'm still the starving ergonomic boy
who bends the innocent sestina in your honor, who, loyal, tends his neutral corner, you shall
        deliver me or suffer, as any minute I may guess which abeyant machinery's name
to call out when it's time to wipe you from the rhetoric of the stage. Have patience: in just
        five minutes we will see
what's come to take you. Recall the rat-snake, last year, hunting in the corn-crib? Stage left,
        we could've let a rat-snake stand for mercy;
backstage, we should've let it stand for nothing: the sky raked open like the sky I'm always
        hoping for in poems, one barn a telepathic warning to go easy; two barns,
        and then I get a little dizzy, and across the fields that night—

snake or no rat-snake—oh Naif, you twirled infirmly. Since then, most nights
I hide the telephone in the dresser; I fear the third barn; and when I open up my mouth
to pray, I refer to you as *The Talent*. Will you demand your name above the title? If so,
        then I shall have to beg you mercy
before I've even mentioned Jesus, himself a healthy, smiling boy
rattling wingless in your jet-stream. Jesus, Ramona, from our vantage point *sub rosa*, I can see
the curve of the earth when you wear those shoes, my name

misspelled on empty crates you shipped to China, your name
a name to hang some grief on while the camouflagéd night banks fiercely, night into night
        like cars into walls, and just tonight
and just like in some lonely barracks, I dreamt we spoke those cyprian words again; I dreamt
        that you could see
into my head, where nowadays, more than ever, how I wish I were a nun, my mouth
scrolling through sentences as vague and inoffensive as music in a hotel lobby, and it's easy
        to think I'm just the pious boy
sent straight from central casting, but you better call me Sister, sister, because I take
        my job seriously, here at the hospital, where my very touch means mercy,

where I count your cock-eyed shoes, sticking up from each and every gurney: mercy, now,
        in highway collision, mercy in the trapdoor mouth (for they have come to take you),
        mercy in those cyprian words which, once spoken, brought you to this
            hotel room where your very touch means mercy.
Oh, Ramona, shoes and all, let's face it: you are the kind of girl whose heart has gone out
        to machines, your name
has gone out ringing doorbells down dusty lanes where I may yet be just a boy.
Your forced disappearance should be simple, but on this stage, even the harder sciences

are love-songs, and something had to leave you here, and something
            now must take you back, on into the cabled night,
where dubious the lightning forks the corners of your mouth,
the sky raked open like the sky I'm always hoping for in poems and darker even than the
            baleful congress of your eyes, two blackened seas

wherein the many Scyllas and Charybdi paper-rock-and-scissor for their sailors, with nary
            a check in their loss column, no Odysseus yet with his tough street credit, and never
                        to look across those blackened seas
and see the fabled sail which puts them, beaten, in the record books. Your eyes *those* kinds of eyes,
            Ramona, printed with monsters and no mercy
but this warning, *Caution, may cause immaculate conception. The third barn is burning
            in her mouth,*
and because you fall so often over North America, we have 41 names
for how your body hits the ground. You are a broadly interpreted religion, an oath sworn
            over car engines in the night.
When I step outside and look across the fields we used to run—when you were still posing
            as a boy,

your self-taught hair casting fish-hook shadows on the barnside—I remember why I left
            this town and left you to the boys
pitching shingles off the farmhouse roof: with you, there was never any way to see
you clearly; with you, there were never telephones enough to say goodbye, and say I laid you
            out along the frontage road one Sunday night
in order to parade your public past you. So what you're longer than the mall? Which mercies
did you come here to dispense? I'm the only one can say your name
and drive it closest to the sound of glass, cracking in the hollow of the mouth:

so open up your mouth, Ramona: pick the perfect spot for trauma: search the ancient list of boys
until you run across my name. Roll it, like machinery, from your tongue, because I'd like to see
you gone if that be mercy: whatever lightning is was *you* again, what clamor raining through
            your heart was night.

Zombie Sunday

Gentle handed holy father, or whomever,
you used to be a classy place,
but allow me, once again, my tender,
adulterated access to the moon, who isn't
getting any younger, who knows a trick or two.
Old, dilated moon, what are you fixing
to deliver, what secrets do you list?
You flinched, and loved the stars, your stepsisters,
who hated you for your proximity,
your ugly, mushroom face a distraction
from their slender, mercenary graces.
You can all but see me. I am old
like you, and the sun, that closest of stars,
has come a hundred thousand years
to burn us to our recognizable teeth.
Let us throw our books together
in one big pile, we are but sad again.
Let me say a few words over you
while you recall the better times
when you were young, and ran with planets.
You have played the shy dove before,
don't lie, greedy for the butch, kamikaze-
posture of comet and meteor, taking
the shock on your dirty heels and listening
to the rapid freelance prayers
which were our way to bed. You were
a thinner dish then, your skirt
in one light hand, your teeth indifferent.
The tunnels below your chalky skin
were vast and populous, yet I have seen you
worse, elongated at the poles of axis
and chewed to a core by time, a juvenile.
How will the dead be raised?
With what bodies will they come?
The green waves you have sculpted for our amusement
retch forth their warm froth onto the brown earth
you didn't, your brief and febrile
memorial, my original lungs anchored
like frogs to a flopping piece of kelp.
You were my own passionate cousin,

my furtive corollary, the logical extension.
I would murder you for money.
They will dredge you from the sky.

Cyborg

Ramona your only eyes
are river-traffic, are fast
and fish-tailing milk,
are troublesome

devices, are difficult
to mimic, but I will design
others like them, I have come
across the parking lot

to tell you this. The world
is dark with invention
and I have mastered
the variable machinery

which moves your only
mouth, I have mastered
the root-path and shad-blue
veins of your hands,

I have lingered awhile
considering
the format of your spine.
I can reproduce you. I know

the river thought so
too, looping out
your living name
across Kentucky,

the foothills blotched
with Orphic vowels
and the consonants sticking
like trees from the river-

bed. All the pilgrims
of Kentucky came
to drink it, it was a name
suited for such

communicable
purposes, the flood-water
contrail of your R
slowing through the flats

of Georgia, picking up
an open red and trailing off
in salt. Like the river
I have worried over each

your every fingernail
but I have taken clippings
and you will grow for me
marketable, many-handed, green-

headed, whole and well
in the flower, and such
is my love that I will sell you
I will mark you up

and down and then
the river will be nothing
but an empty fist
and even that is not

enough, so I have had
to invent the river
who has never
known you. I had nothing

to go on. No model
to guide me. I am
a genius. I'll need
to burn you ten

more times. Twenty
more hands, please, ten
more mouths, your
hair dispatched, sub-

marine-like and prohibitive
through the gears
of axis, and you
have gotten into

everything, the cupboards,
the insides
of rocks, the water-
table, the compass

pulses slightly when
I read the sentences
you left behind
in books, the tree-top

Ts and Ls flat-
lining into
your anonymous
lower cases—you always

helped me feel so
sick, so poor—I cannot
wrangle with you in
my sleep, I cannot

spell *heartache* with
so much trouble in
the world or was it with
your church shoes

in my hand? But you
don't have a choice
you are coming back
regardless; there is

so much for you
to do. Penance. Time.
I've revised the blueprints.
I've sold the space

on the inside of your
left arm. I have registered
your coenesthesis—I
can't imagine that

your eyes will weigh
too much—and I am sorry,
love, that my science
will not fail me.

A Note on the Type

An elegant, refreshing English linotype designed by the Red Nun of Prague, Sister Anna Maria Cornucopia, in the year 1456, this typeface was weaned on the Gutenberg Bible, beaten as a child, abandoned to earn a living on the mean streets of Barcelona, put in the stocks for coveting its neighbor's sheep and sleeping with anything, stoned by royalty, drunk by noon, excommunicated to Capri but shipwrecked on Ithaka, bred up Homeric, adopted by wolves, soon adolesced into apocalypse and petty exhibitionism, was card shark, known foot-fetishist having characteristics of the Bulmer and Baskerville, but with a distinguished profile of its own— reminding one of the clouds that pass across the sun, or a hearse pulling up to the drive thru—was linked romantically to Vasco Da Gama, had a good singing voice, poked John Milton with a spoon, denied involvement in several attempts on the life of the last remaining dodo, put dolphins to work, taught the facts of life to a Spaniard, offered up handkerchiefs when John Keats cried, once used to brand the words *Never Again* across an Antibean gigolo's backside (also available in paperback), was versatile member of Parliament, known fencer, *agent frotteur*, tried its hand at cricket, was lost to history for a hundred years before popping up as a trapper in Wisconsin, traveled widely, gave Emily Dickinson a piece of its mind, was 16th wife of the lost Sheik of Memphis, Tennessee, 5th degree black-belt, snappy dresser, bird-dogger, roustabout, mammy-rammer, jack-roller, inventor of jelly, later shot Billy the Kid, moonlit as well-digger, called in to smooth things over between Rimbaud and Verlaines, mispronounced French names, was shot in WWI and now has a funny looking "F," broke up Scott Fitzgerald at parties, french kissed Gertrude Stein, danced before Hitler, was dusted for the fingerprints of Jesus and TS Eliot, burned books, ran for mayor, coined the phrase *arid archipelago of loss*, went down over Hanoi like a minister going down on his child bride, left the lid off the mayo, was credited with the writing of Virginia sodomy laws, moved to California where it picked up its tannic aftertaste and Joan Baez, changed its name to Slick, knocked out Mike Tyson in the 1st round, ran guns to Castro and Budweiser to Boy Scout Troop #9, fell on hard times, held up a convenience store in Fresno, white, six feet tall, Shakespeare's sonnet #58 tattooed on the inside of its cheek, last used in ransom note asking 12 dollars for the un-dismembered body of the reader and wanted, so bad that we can taste it, for the obscene and inarticulate trafficking of the moon.